Understanding Nonprofit Financial Statements (in 30 Pages)

~

A Short Tutorial for Board, Management, & Staff

Thomas R. Ittelson

MercuryGroupPress
Cambridge, Massachusetts

**Understanding Nonprofit Financial Statements in 30 Pages:
A Short Tutorial for Board, Management and Staff**

Copyright © 2020 by Thomas Ittelson

Available in quantity from the Publisher.

ISBN: 978-1-970050-40-0

MercuryGroupPress
P.O. Box 381350
Cambridge, MA 02238
www.mercurygrouppress.com
financialstatements@mercurygrouppress.com
617-285-1168

Library of Congress Cataloging-in-Publication Data

Available upon request.

Limits of Liability & Disclaimer of Warranty: The author is not an accountant nor an attorney and does not represent himself as either. The publisher and the author have attempted to make diligent efforts in preparing this book. However, they make no representations or warranties with respect to the accuracy or completeness of the contents of this book and specifically disclaim any implied warranties of merchantability or fitness for a particular purpose. The advice and strategies contained herein may not be suitable for your situation. You should consult with an accountant, attorney or other appropriate professional where appropriate. Neither the publisher nor the author shall be liable for any loss of profit or any other commercial damages, including but not limited to special, incidental, consequential or other damages.

Contents

Money is most often the nonprofit organization's scarcest resource. How well money is used is the best measure of board, management, and, staff performance. Financial statements show that performance.

Board members and non-financial managers do not need to be accountants or financial experts. They should, however, understand financial statements and reports that their organization regularly produces to document mission success.

Most important decisions made by nonprofit organizations are based, in some material way, on accounting information. Efficient and effective stewardship of monies received in support of mission is the gold standard by which to measure all performance in nonprofits.

Introduction

Virtually every decision a nonprofit organization makes has its roots in accounting information. While many board members, managers, and staff may lack a background in accounting and finance, they should have a basic understanding of their organization's financial underpinnings. This short book will guide readers through the fundamentals of nonprofit accounting, financial statements, and financial reporting.

Accounting is record keeping; the accounting rules describe how the records should be kept. Accounting rules are formulated by the *Financial Accounting Standards Board* (FASB) and are called *Generally Accepted Accounting Principles* (GAAP).

Financial Statements are summaries of the financial transactions of an organization over time. The four major nonprofit statements (and their for-profit equivalents) are the *Statements of Activities* (Income Statement), the *Statement of Financial Position* (Balance Sheet), the *Statement of Cash Flows*, and the *Statement of Functional Expenses (only for nonprofits).*

Financial Reporting is presenting your accounting records and statements in a form that you and other people can understand. Nonprofit organizations must file this information in IRS Form 990 each year. See page 23 for a description of this form.

~

Nonprofit accounting and financial reporting are different in purpose and scope from that in profit making companies. Nonprofit organizations are not organized to make a profit. This fundamental difference is reflected in the accounting and reporting setup for nonprofits. The focus in this book will be on the special accounting treatments for nonprofit contributions, gifts, grants, contracts, and program services revenue and expense — highlighting the key differences between accounting in nonprofit organizations and in for-profit companies.

Hint, the biggest differences are in the definitions of revenue and profit (called surplus in nonprofit organizations) and when and how they are recorded and reported.

The Nonprofit World

Almost all the 1,600,000 or so nonprofit organizations in the U.S. are state-chartered corporations and must register as such with the Secretary of State in each state where they operate and raise funds (a very few nonprofits such as the American Red Cross and the Boy Scouts of America, are federally chartered).

All nonprofit organizations must have a specific, approved public purpose (mission) and they do not have "owners" in the traditional sense. They are held as a public trust and governed by a voluntary board of directors.

Nonprofits employ over 10% (16 million people) of the U.S. workforce and an additional 25% (60 million people) are active volunteers. Nonprofits represent over $1 trillion to the U.S. economy, which is over 5% of the Gross Domestic Product (GDP).

Public Charities: (501(c)(3) Organizations

Nonprofit "public charities" accept tax-deductible contributions. The designation "501(c)(3)" refers to the section of the IRS tax code describing these organization. Charities include most organizations active in the arts, education, health care, and human services. Religious congregations are also considered public charities, but for constitutional reasons they are not required to register with the IRS.

Over 60% of all American households donate to nonprofit organizations, over $400 billion in 2019. And, when you think about it, government does its own charitable giving in the form of allowing tax deductions to individuals when they give to qualified charities.

When an individual donates to a charity, the federal government essentially pays a portion of that donation. A $1,000 donation from a donor in the highest income-tax bracket, costs the donor only about $600 in cash. the federal government kicks in the remaining $400 in the form of a reduction in the donor's taxes. The nonprofit receives the full $1,000 in cash.

Some Basic Accounting Principles

Accountants have some basic rules and assumptions upon which rest all their work in preparing financial statements. These accounting rules and assumptions dictate what financial items to measure and when and how to measure them. Here are some of the most relevant rules:

Note, accounting is simply record keeping and the accounting rules describe how these records should be kept. financial statements in the U.S. must be prepared according to the accounting profession's set of rules and guiding principles called the *Generally Accepted Accounting Principles,* GAAP for short. We have listed some of them below. GAAP is a series of conventions, rules and procedures for preparing and reporting financial statements. The *Financial Accounting Standards Board,* FASB for short, lays out the GAAP conventions, rules and procedures. The FASB's mission is "to establish and improve standards of financial accounting and reporting for guidance and education of the public, including issuers, auditors, and users of financial information."

CPAs Who are the people who make these rules? Certified Public Accountants (CPAs) make the rules. They have been specially trained in college and have practiced auditing of organizations for a number of years. In addition, they have passed a series of exams testing their clear understanding of both accounting principles and auditing procedures. Note that FASB is made up mostly of CPAs and that CPAs both develop, interpret and apply GAAP when they audit an organization. All this is fairly incestuous.

Some important rules relevant to nonprofits:

Measurement Accounting deals with things that can be quantified — resources and obligations upon which there is an agreed-upon value. Accounting only deals with things that can be measured. This measurement assumption leaves out many very valuable "assets." For example, loyal donors, competent staff, volunteer efforts, and so forth.

Materiality Materiality refers to the relative importance of different financial information. Accountants don't sweat the small stuff. But all transactions must be reported if they would materially affect the financial condition of the organization.

Remember, what is material for a neighborhood social services organization is not material for the American Red Cross (lost in the rounding errors). Materiality is a straightforward judgment call.

Estimates and Judgements Complexity and uncertainty make any measurement less than exact. Estimates and judgments must often be made for financial reporting. It is okay to guess if: (a) that is the best you can do, and (b) the expected error would not matter much anyway. But your financial folks should use the same guessing method for each period. Be consistent in your guesses and do the best you can.

Consistency Sometimes identical transactions can be accounted for differently. You could do it this way or that way, depending upon some preference. The principle of consistency states that each individual organization must choose a single method of reporting and use it consistently over time. You cannot switch back and forth. Measurement techniques must be the same from any one fiscal period to another.

Conservatism Accountants have a downward measurement bias, preferring understatement to overvaluation. Hopefully, fewer "negative surprises" will occur than with more aggressive reporting.

Periodicity Accountants assume that the life of a corporation can be divided into periods of time for which revenue and surplus can be reported, usually a month, quarter or year. What is so special about a month, quarter or year? Well, they are just convenient periods; short enough so that management can remember what has happened, long enough to have meaning and not just be random fluctuations.

These periods are called "fiscal" periods. For example, a "fiscal year" could extend from October 1 in one year till September 30 in the next year. Often nonprofits use fiscal years different than a calendar year since those audits tend to be cheaper.

Fiduciary Duty

Fiduciary duty requires nonprofit board members to make careful, good-faith decisions in the best interest of the organization, consistent with its public or charitable mission and independent of undue influence of any party or from their own financial self-interest. These duties apply to management and staff as well.

Financial Fraud

If proper financial controls are not in place in a nonprofit organization, financial fraud by trusted employees is a ticking time bomb. An organization is most susceptible to financial fraud if it has inadequate systems and procedures, lax controls with few checks and balances, no outside accountants, and then it compounds the problem by looking the other away. *Sound familiar?*

See page 31 for the author's new book on nonprofit fraud!

Nonprofit Financial Statements

Four financial statements present the financial condition of a nonprofit organization. They summarize the financial impact of the organizations efforts toward achieving its stated mission. The financial statements of nonprofits are publicly distributed for everyone to see and analyze. We will describe each statement in turn and then show how they present a true financial picture of the organization. It's not rocket science. *Read on...*

1. The nonprofit *Statement of Activities* shows money coming into the organization (revenue) and money going out (expenses) for a specific period. It is analogous to the *Income Statement* of for-profit companies.

Revenue – Expenses = Change in Net Assets

2. The nonprofit *Statement of Financial Position* shows what the organization owns (assets),what it owes (liabilities), and it's worth. It is analogous to a for-profit *Balance Sheet.*

Assets = Liabilities + Net Assets

3. The *Cash Flow Statements* shows the organization's cash balance at the start of a period and at the end of the period Both the nonprofit and for-profit statements are similar.

Beginning Cash + Cash-In – Cash-Out = Ending Cash

4. A fourth statement, the *Statement of Functional Expenses,* is unique to nonprofit reporting. It documents the organization's expenses by program.

~

Most nonprofit organizations keep their books on an "accrual basis." That means, (a) when revenue is received (or pledged) it is recorded on the financial statements, and (b) expense is recorded when the organization has incurred an obligation to pay, whether or not cash has changed hands. Only small nonprofits may keep their books on a simpler "cash basis." In cash basis accounting, transactions are recorded when cash comes in or cash goes out.

STATEMENT OF ACTIVITIES *(for the period)*

REVENUE	WITHOUT DONOR RESTRICTIONS	② WITH DONOR RESTRICTIONS		
① CONTRIBUTIONS & GIFTS			$	0
PROGRAM SERVICES REVENUE				0
GRANTS & CONTRACTS				0
OTHER REVENUE				0
TOTAL REVENUE	$ 0	$0	$	0
EXPENSES				
FUNDRAISING				0
③ PROGRAM SERVICES				0
GRANTS & CONTRACTS				0
MANAGEMENT & GENERAL				0
TOTAL EXPENSES	$ 0		$	0
CHANGE IN NET ASSETS			$	0
④ **BEGINNING NET ASSETS**				0
ENDING NET ASSETS			$	0

Revenue – Expenses = Change in Net Assets
— for the period —

Note: Numeric entries are made only in the boxed [   ] elements shown on the sample statements above and on pages 10, 13, and 14. The totals shown are additions or subtractions of the boxed elements as appropriate. For example, *Total Revenue* minus *Total Expenses* equals *Change in Net Assets*.

Acronyms: As in other specialized fields, accounting uses acronyms and abbreviations to speed and simplify discussions. Here are important ones: *G&A* — general and administrative, as in G&A expense. *SG&A* — sales, general and administrative, as in SG&A expense, *PP&E* — property, plant, and equipment (fixed assets).

"Net" means after deductions, whereas "gross" means before taking deductions. For example, "net fixed assets" means fixed asset @ cost minus depreciation charges.

Statement 1. Statement of Activities

The money left over when you subtract expenses from revenue for a nonprofit organization is called "surplus" or, more formally stated, the organization's *Change in Net Assets* over a specified period of time. The term, *Net Assets* is unique to nonprofit accounting and is analogous to a for-profit company's shareholders' equity on its *Income Statement*.

① Nonprofit revenue is all the money coming into the organization during the period (plus pledges to contribute in the future). Revenue is shown on the *Statement of Activities* and categorized by type:

Contributions & Gifts are recorded in the *Statement of Activities* when cash is received from a donor or a donor makes a promise (pledge) to give cash in the future.

Pledges to nonprofit organizations are handled in a very special way. They are recognized as revenue when the pledge is made, not when money is actually received.

Contributions and gifts (and pledges, when funded) are tax deductible by the donor when given to 501(c)(3) public charities. Receipts must be provided to donors for contributions of $250 or more.

Program Services Revenue is recorded when the nonprofit organization provides a product or service to a client for a fee. This transfer of product or service for money is often called an "exchange transaction." The nonprofit organization exchanges its products or services for cash paid by the receiver of the products or services.

Just because goods and services can be purchased from a nonprofit organization, does not mean that the nonprofit organization is jeopardizing its nonprofit status. Nonprofit organizations often sell goods and services that support their public mission. The nonprofit organization may even generate an increase in *Net Assets* (surplus) in the transaction, analogous to profit for a for-profit company. More later.

Grants & Contracts is revenue from institutional donors such as governmental agencies, other charitable organizations, and foundations. These grants and contracts are usually: (a) for a specific stated purpose, (b) to be performed in a specific period of time, and (c) directly related to the recipient nonprofit organization's skills and charitable mission.

Other Revenue is revenue received from sources other than those listed as separate line items. but, if revenue from a source type is large, it really should have its own line on the *Statement of Activities*. Membership fees, ticket sales, auction proceeds, revenue from special events, advertisement sales, contributed goods or services (at fair market value), and so forth, are examples of other types of revenue.

② *Nonprofit Revenue Restrictions* Revenue is classified on the *Statement of Activities* in two groupings depending on whether any use restrictions are placed on the contribution by the donor:

1. **Without Donor Restrictions** (unrestricted revenue). The organization can use this revenue for any mission purpose at the discretion of the board.

2, **With Donor Restrictions** (restricted revenue). The organization can only use this revenue for the specific purpose (and time period) specified by the donor (and accepted by the board).

Prior to changes in nonprofit accounting practice in 2017, the restricted category of endowments (only interest received can be spent) was a separate category. Now endowments are just presented in the restricted revenue bucket.

③ *Nonprofit Expenses* Expenses shown on the *Statement Activities* are grouped into specific categories:

Fundraising expenses are expenditures to solicit contributions, gifts, contracts, and grants.

Program Services expenses are expenditures to deliver goods and services to clients in support of mission. Salaries and wages are often the biggest expense here.

Grants & Contracts expenses are expenditures to fulfill the requirements of government and foundation contracts in support of the organization's mission.

Management & General expenses (sometimes called overhead) are for occupancy, utilities, general management, accounting, legal, and other "keeping the doors open" functions and are essential for a well-functioning organization. Sometimes nonprofits skimp on these necessary expenditures. Sometimes granting agencies will not cover them. Sigh.

④ Notice the change, beginning, and ending *Net Assets* lines at the bottom of the *Statement of Activities*.

Change in Net Assets is simply the difference between the nonprofit organization's revenues and expenses for the period, often called surplus. This amount is analogous to profit in a for-profit company,

Beginning Net Assets is the accumulated annual changes in net assets since the nonprofit's inception. We reported this amount as the *Ending Net Assets* for the prior period. *Beginning Net Assets* plus *Change in Net Assets* equals ***Ending Net Assets*** for this reporting period.

Note: The net assets of nonprofit organizations and profits of for-profit companies differ in that net assets belong to the organization itself and may only be used by the organization in support of its public mission. In contrast, all the profits made by a for-profit company belong to its shareholders (owners). These profits are available for distribution as dividends to these shareholders. But since nonprofit organizations have no "owners" they can make no such distributions and all surplus is retained by the organization to be used in furtherance of its mission.

STATEMENT OF FINANCIAL POSITION *(as of the period ending date)*

ASSETS

CASH		
ACCOUNTS RECEIVABLE		
⑤ INVENTORIES		
PREPAID EXPENSES		
PLEDGES RECEIVABLE		
INVESTMENTS		
PP&E (NET)		
TOTAL ASSETS	$	0

LIABILITIES & NET ASSETS

ACCOUNTS PAYABLE		
SHORT TERM DEBT		
⑥ LONG TERM DEBT		
ACCRUED EXPENSES		
NET ASSETS:		
⑦ W/O DONOR RESTRICTIONS		
WITH DONOR RESTRICTIONS		
TOTAL LIABILITIES & NET ASSETS	$	0

Total Assets = Total Liabilities + Net Assets
— at the end of a period, a moment in time —

Note: Total Assets will always equal total Liabilities plus Net Assets according to the basic equation of Accounting — *What you Own – What you Owe = What you're Worth* — rearranged and then presented in the *Statement of Financial Position.*

Statement 2: Statement of Financial Position

The *Statement of Financial Position* of a nonprofit organization shows the organization's financial strength at a single point in time, commonly reported at the end of a year. It is analogous to a for-profit company's *Balance Sheet.* The statement presents:

(a) *Assets* — what the organization owns,

(b) *Liabilities* — what the organization owes others, and

(c) *Net Assets* — what the organization is worth.

⑤ *Assets* are everything the organization owns — cash in the bank, inventory, equipment, buildings — all of it. Assets are also certain "rights" that have a monetary value such as *Collections Receivable* from donors who have pledged contributions but have yet to fund them. *Prepaid Expenses* (services paid for by the organization but not yet used) are also included in assets.

The different asset types are listed on the *Statement of Financial Position* in order of descending liquidity — the speed with which each type of asset can be turned into actual dollars and cents. *Cash* is at the top of the liquidity list. Land and buildings are at the bottom of the list, taking the longest to turn into cash.

⑥ *Liabilities* are financial obligations of the organization, such as money it owes to lenders, to suppliers, to employees, and to others. Liabilities are listed by type in the *Liabilities & Net Assets* section of the *Statement of Financial Position* and ordered by how soon they will need to be paid. If the values of individual categories are large, they would be shown on separate lines.

Accounts Payable and the current portion of debt are referred to as the organization's **Current Liabilities.** Current liabilities will be paid-off within the next 12 months with cash generated by the organization collecting its **Current Assets** *(Cash, Accounts Receivable, Inventories, Prepaid Expenses,* and *Contributions Receivable).*

⑦ *Net Assets* can be thought of as a special obligation of the organization to be used to serve its mission. It represents the unspent wealth (revenue minus expenses) accumulated since the founding of the organization. Net Assets are presented on the statement separately by restriction category.

Unrestricted Net Assets are contributions and gifts that the organization can use for any purpose to further its mission.

Unrestricted Revenue (the source of *Unrestricted Net Assets*) is the unconditional, nonreciprocal transfer of assets by a donor to a nonprofit organization. Once given, the donor cannot take the money back and cannot dictate its use.

Restricted Net Assets are the portion of *Net Assets* of the organization the use of which is limited by donor-imposed conditions. *Restricted Net Assets* will become **Unrestricted Net Assets** when the stated restrictions expire with time or are fulfilled by the actions of the organization. The value of nonprofit organization's *restricted net assets* is always in flux.

Donor-imposed use restrictions specify how the donor wants donated money to be spent. These restrictions are contractual requirements that organizations perform a specific program at a specific time in the future. An **endowment** is a special type of *restricted net asset* but that can never be spent.

Statement 3. Nonprofit Statement of Cash Flows

The *Statement of Cash Flows* is just like your checkbook register. You subtract an amount when you spend money and add an amount when you receive and deposit money. Every month (hopefully!) you tally all your entries and reconcile the checkbook.

A positive cash flow for a period means that the organization has more cash at the end of the period than at its beginning. A negative cash flow for a period means that the organization has less cash at the end of the period than at its beginning.

A continuing negative cash flow may mean that the organization is approaching financial difficulties and even bankruptcy.

STATEMENT OF CASH FLOWS	*for the period*
BEGINNING CASH	$ 0
CASH RECEIPTS	
CASH DISBURSEMENTS	
CASH FLOW FROM OPERATIONS	$ 0
PP&E PURCHASES	
NET BORROWINGS	
INVESTMENT INCOME	
ENDING CASH	$ 0

Beginning Cash + Cash Inflows − Cash Outflows = Ending Cash
— for the period —

STATEMENT OF FUNCTIONAL EXPENSES *(for the period)*

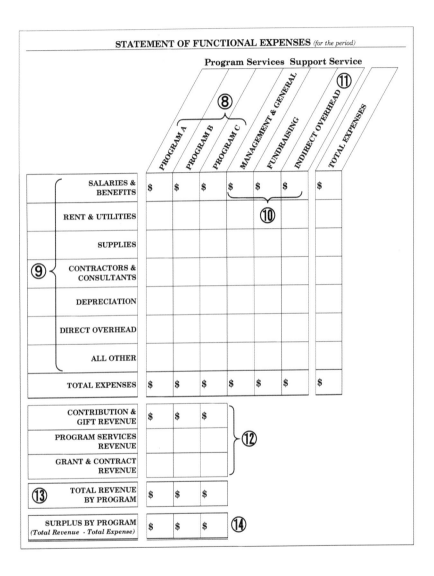

| | Program Services | | | Support Service | | | |
	PROGRAM A	PROGRAM B	PROGRAM C ⑧	MANAGEMENT & GENERAL	FUNDRAISING	INDIRECT OVERHEAD	TOTAL EXPENSES ⑪
SALARIES & BENEFITS	$	$	$	$	$	$ ⑩	$
RENT & UTILITIES							
SUPPLIES							
⑨ CONTRACTORS & CONSULTANTS							
DEPRECIATION							
DIRECT OVERHEAD							
ALL OTHER							
TOTAL EXPENSES	$	$	$	$	$	$	$
CONTRIBUTION & GIFT REVENUE	$	$	$				
PROGRAM SERVICES REVENUE				⑫			
GRANT & CONTRACT REVENUE							
⑬ TOTAL REVENUE BY PROGRAM	$	$	$				
SURPLUS BY PROGRAM *(Total Revenue - Total Expense)*	$	$	$	⑭			

Statement 4. Nonprofit Statement of Functional Expenses

This IRS required statement, unique to nonprofits, presents the organization's expenses in greater detail than is shown on the *Statement of Activities*. A matrix format is used presenting two classes of expenses:

- *"natural"* expenses in rows grouped by salaries, benefits, supplies, and so forth, versus
- *"functional"* expenses in columns grouped by specific program services projects and also showing internal support services.

Natural expenses are grouped according to type. *Functional expenses* are grouped according to the purpose for which costs are incurred. This matrix presentation highlights both direct and indirect overhead expenses in a straightforward and informative way.

Note, while not required by GAAP or the IRS, adding revenue totals at the bottom of the matrix will show surplus generated by a specific program and allow for a program-expense ratio (described on page 18) to be calculated for the program.

⑧ *Programs* Most nonprofit organizations administer several standalone, though most often interrelated, programs. It is often useful to look at their financials separately and the *Statement of Functional Expenses* does just that. *Functional Expense Groups* Reporting by these groupings shows the organization's expenditures by major programs. Is the organization's spending congruent with its mission? Is it putting its money where its mouth is?

⑨ *Natural Expense Groups* Reporting by these groupings shows the organization's expenditures by the type of expense — how it spends its money to get desired results. Is this allocation of expenses the most efficient and effective mix?

Overhead Overhead expenses are often viewed with suspicion by donors and other funders as a potential waste of money. However, these expenses are real (rent, utilities, audits, finance, staff training and so forth) and are required in a well-managed organization. Classification of overhead as support services, direct overhead and indirect overhead, provides more information and additional clarity to these important and necessary expenses.

⑩ Support Service Allocations Some overhead expenses are best thought of as organization-wide, such as the CEO's salary. Others can be assigned to a specific program as direct overhead, such as occupancy and other space costs used by the program.

⑪ Indirect Overhead Indirect overhead is an expense that is difficult to assign to specific project or functional expense group. An example would be liability insurance for the board of directors.

⑫ Direct Overhead Direct overhead can be assigned but is really of an "all-other" type and does not fit into a natural expense group. An example would be insurance for a building exclusively used by a specific program.

⑬ Revenue by Program As it prepares budgets, the board must decide and allocate by program how the unrestricted contribution and gift revenue will be used. Restricted contributions, grant revenue, and contact revenue is easy to record by program once it is spent. Program services revenue is recorded by program when performed.

⑭ Surplus by Program Revenue minus expense equals surplus. Is the organization generating a surplus in all its programs? Is one program showing a large loss, and can we justify this loss? This data line summarizes surplus generated by separate programs.

Fund Accounting

Since restricted revenue must be earmarked for the donor's stated gift purpose, nonprofit organizations account separately for expenses by each program funded. This special process is called **"fund accounting."** The requirement to segregate restricted contributions and gifts and their associated expenses adds a complexity to a nonprofit's accounting that is not found in for-profit organization.

When a nonprofit organization accepts restricted revenue, it forms a commercial "contract" with the donor requiring it to spend the revenue as described in that contract. Auditors and the IRS require that the nonprofit organization document this restricted use in its books and attest to only spending the money from the donors for their intended purpose. Donors can sue for recovery of the donation if misused and it is a felony to expropriate the funds by spending them for any other purpose.

Note, the summary financial statements described in this book only show the total of restricted revenue and of restricted funds spent for all of the organizations active restricted projects. Separate accounting schedules document total revenue minus expenses for each specific project and show the "funds balance" available for future expenditures for that project

∼

Interestingly, an organization can have lots of restricted-use cash on hand while also being cash-starved. Restricted-use cash can't be spent for other purposes and is effectively "frozen," not helping to provide necessary liquidity to the organization. For this reason, nonprofit managements actively seek and highly value unrestricted contributions.

Most important decisions made by non-profit organizations are based, in some material way, on accounting decisions.

Efficient and effective stewardship of monies received in support of mission is the gold standard by which to measure all performance in non-profits.

Financial Ratio Analysis

As a board member or non-financial manager, it is important to understand how to use financial statements in understanding the financial health of the organization. A good way to analyze financial statements is through ratios: in other words, comparing two numbers with each other.

Following is a discussion of financial ratios specifically useful in gauging a nonprofit organization's performance. Note also, most of the financial ratios used for for-profit companies are applicable to nonprofit organizations as well.

Fundraising Expense Ratio is the *Fundraising Expense* divided by *Revenue*. Values of 10% to 30% are normal, depending on the type of solicitation, how well established the organization, and the organization's fundraising aggressiveness.

$$\text{Fundraising Expense Ratio} = \frac{\text{Fundraising Expense}}{\text{Revenue}}$$

Return on Revenue is a standard profitability ratio computed as increase in *Net Assets* divided by *Revenue* for the period. I know, I know, nonprofit organizations do not generate profits as do for-profit companies. However, nonprofits have the analogous, *Change in Net Assets* (revenue minus expenses) that is called a nonprofit **"surplus."** Achieving a surplus is necessary to grow the size and scope of nonprofit organizations by providing capital. Consistent surplus generation indicates strong financial management of the organization. A 2% to 3% surplus is a good target. Surplus provides that cushion to ride out a slow donation period or to seize a strategic opportunity.

$$\text{Return on Revenue} = \frac{\text{Surplus}}{\text{Revenue}}$$

Revenue Reliance Ratio measures how many of your eggs are being carried in one basket. Below 33% is a good target. Mostly relying on a single income source is risky because it could go away and leave you with nothing to fall back on. Lower overall risk to the organization's long-term viability is found with a broad base of support from individuals, foundations, and government agencies through contributions and gifts, program services revenue, contracts, and grants.

$$\text{Revenue Reliance Ratio} = \frac{\text{Revenue from Largest Source}}{\text{Total Revenue}}$$

Self-Sufficiency Ratio measures *Program Services Revenue* divided by *Total Revenue*. A high ratio means the organization generates enough revenue on its own through program services to sustain itself without gifts and grants.

$$\text{Self Sufficiency Ratio} = \frac{\text{Program Services Revenue}}{\text{Total Revenue}}$$

Overhead Ratio is the percentage of a nonprofit's expenses for *Fundraising* plus *General & Management Expenses* relative to its *Total Expenses*. There is no "right" percentage here, 15% to 30% is common. administrative expenses often account for 10% of revenue, while fundraising can account for between 5% to 20% depending on fundraising strategy and how established is the organization.

$$\text{Overhead Ratio} = \frac{\text{Fundraising} + \text{Management \& General Expense}}{\text{Total Expenses}}$$

Organizations have different strategies of operation and function in different realms. Donors scrutinize the overhead ratio for waste and inefficiency. However, we all can agree that the fundraising and administrative expenses are essential to sustaining the organization. How much to spend, however, is a continuing debate and a management judgement call.

The **Program Expense Ratio**, the mirror of the *Overhead Ratio*, is the percentage of direct program services expense to total expenses. Generally, the higher the better.

$$\text{Program Expense Ratio} = \frac{\text{Program Expense}}{\text{Total Expenses}}$$

KPIs & Dashboards

Financial statements are not the only option for presenting financial information and examples of mission success. Nonprofit organizations must measure performance to mission with both words and numbers. For-profit companies have a single ultimate measure of success, profits! Things are not so simple for nonprofit organizations. Key questions for nonprofits to ask and then to answer are:

- Overall, how healthy is our organization today? Is it healthier today than it was three years ago? Why or why not?

- Are our programs sustainable, that is, generating the resources required to meet today's needs without compromising the future?

This book focuses mostly on financial measures of success. Note that an organization faithfully adhering to its mission, but operating with sloppy resource and financial management, is failing. However, also note that a beautifully run financial operation that strays from its mission is also failing.

Key Performance Indicators KPIs are quantifiable measurements as well as qualitative written descriptions of a nonprofit organization's health and success. An organization's KPIs are usually benchmarked against peer organizations and commonly recognized business-model ratios.

Different types of nonprofit organizations will use different KPIs. For example: contribution & gift revenue growth compared to fundraising expense, visitor and membership data for a museum, enrollment data for a day care center, number of patients served for a clinic, and so forth.

Dashboards Graphic "dashboards" are an ideal way to concisely present these KPIs to stakeholders of the organization. Stakeholders need to know, and they do care! Dashboards are a simple, often colorful, graphic representation of KPIs. With dashboards, performance to mission can be seen at a glance and historical trends — both favorable and unfavorable — are obvious.

Dashboard presentations convey financial and operating information in an easy to understand and difficult to ignore or misinterpret format, riveting attention to what is truly important for the organization and demanding action. See example below.

Graphic Dashboard Example — Report on KPIs

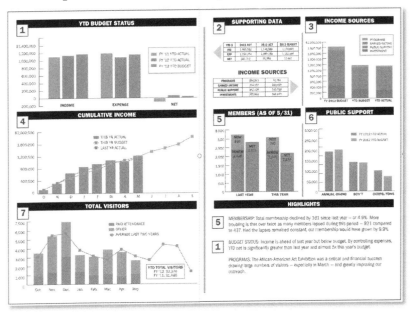

Dashboards do not present as much detailed information as do traditional financial statements. But when used with carefully selected KPIs, they are the best way to communicate critical organization information to nonprofit stakeholders. Every organization should use them.

IRS Reporting with Form 990

Nonprofit organizations report their financial results to the federal government annually using **IRS Form 990**. If you do not file, the organization could lose its nonprofit status. It is important to do it right. It is the law.

In contrast to an individual's income tax form, IRS Form 1040, or a for-profit company's IRS Form 1120 — both of which are private and confidential — a nonprofit organization's Form 990 is available for public observation at the nonprofit's offices and on the internet. There will be many people looking over your shoulder at the filings.

The nonprofit IRS reporting forms come in different flavors for different sizes and types of nonprofit organizations. Use the original **Form 990** for organizations with annual revenue of over $200,000 or total assets over $500,000. While the actual return is only 16 pages long, with required schedules and descriptive narrative, the filing can easily reach over 75 pages.

Form 990-EZ is simpler and can be used by organizations with annual revenue of less than $200,000 and total net assets of less than $500,000. An even simpler form, **Form 990-N** (called the e-Postcard), can be used by small organizations with annual revenue of less than $50,000.

In addition to requiring exhaustive financial information, the Form 990 requires organizations to disclose significant information about their governance procedures and policies, governing documents, relationships with their organization leaders and with third parties, officer's salaries, and more.

Uses of Form 990

Many different groups and individuals use the organization's Form 990 for various purposes. One such use is the staff looking at *"Part VII Compensation of Officers, Directors, Key Employees"* to see what the boss makes!

The IRS uses Form 990 information to assess the organization's compliance with applicable tax laws. Charity "watchdog" groups use information in Form 990 to evaluate and rate nonprofit organizations on efficiency and effectiveness. Grant funding organizations and donors review the ratings of such watchdog groups. The highly public nature of Form 990 presents an opportunity for the organization to share positive information about: (a) its mission and purpose, (b) the positive impact of its activities, and (c) the effectiveness of its programs. Free publicity!

See the contents of the IRS Form 990 below and on the following pages: see the cover and other important financial pages in the Form 990 filing. .

FORM 990: Return of Organization Exempt from Income Tax — Filing Tax Year, Organization's legal name, address, and telephone number, Employer Identification Number (assigned by IRS), Principal officer's name and address

Part I Summary.— Brief description of mission, governance, most significant activities, volunteers, revenue, and expenses

Part II Signature Block — Officer signature and paid-preparer signature

Part III Statement of Program Service Accomplishments — Program descriptions and revenue, expense, and grants summaries

Part IV Checklist of Required Schedules — Commonly filed schedules will vary by organization type, for example:

Schedule A. Public Charity Status and Public Support
Schedule B. Contributors
Schedule C. Political Campaign and Lobbying Activities
Schedule D. Supplemental Financial Statements
Schedule G. Information Regarding Fundraising or Gaming
Schedule J. Compensation Information
Schedule M. Noncash Contributions
Schedule O. Program and Mission Details

Part V. IRS Filings and Tax Compliance

Part VI. Governance, Management, and Disclosure

Part VII Compensation of Officers, Directors, and Key Employees

Part VIII. Statement of Revenue — Revenue amount by type: (a) Contributions, (b) gifts, and fundraising events revenue, (c) Program service revenue, (d) Foundation grants and contracts, (e) Government grants and contracts, (f) Noncash income, (g) Investment income, and (h) Other revenue.

Part IX. Statement of Functional Expenses — Expense amount by type and by function: (a) Program service, (b) Management & general overhead, and (c) Fundraising

Part X. Balance Sheet — Assets, Liabilities & Net assets

Part XI Financial Statements Preparation and Reporting — Accounting method used, cash or accrual? Statements compiled, reviewed, or audited by independent accountant?

Form 990 Summary and Signature Page

Form **990**	**Return of Organization Exempt From Income Tax**	OMB No. 1545-0047
	Under section 501(c), 527, or 4947(a)(1) of the Internal Revenue Code (except private foundations)	**2015**
Department of the Treasury Internal Revenue Service	▶ Do not enter social security numbers on this form as it may be made public. ▶ Information about Form 990 and its instructions is at www.irs.gov/form990.	Open to Public Inspection

A For the 2015 calendar year, or tax year beginning _____, 2015, and ending _____, 20___

B Check if applicable:	C Name of organization	D Employer identification number
☐ Address change	Doing business as	
☐ Name change	Number and street (or P.O. box if mail is not delivered to street address) Room/suite	E Telephone number
☐ Initial return		
☐ Final return/terminated	City or town, state or province, country, and ZIP or foreign postal code	
☐ Amended return		G Gross receipts $
☐ Application pending	F Name and address of principal officer:	H(a) Is this a group return for subordinates? ☐ Yes ☐ No
		H(b) Are all subordinates included? ☐ Yes ☐ No
		If "No," attach a list. (see instructions)

I Tax-exempt status: ☐ 501(c)(3) ☐ 501(c)( )◀ (insert no.) ☐ 4947(a)(1) or ☐ 527

J Website: ▶   H(c) Group exemption number ▶

K Form of organization: ☐ Corporation ☐ Trust ☐ Association ☐ Other ▶   L Year of formation: M State of legal domicile:

Part I Summary

Activities & Governance	1	Briefly describe the organization's mission or most significant activities:	
	2	Check this box ▶ ☐ if the organization discontinued its operations or disposed of more than 25% of its net assets.	
	3	Number of voting members of the governing body (Part VI, line 1a)	3
	4	Number of independent voting members of the governing body (Part VI, line 1b) . . .	4
	5	Total number of individuals employed in calendar year 2015 (Part V, line 2a) . . .	5
	6	Total number of volunteers (estimate if necessary)	6
	7a	Total unrelated business revenue from Part VIII, column (C), line 12	7a
	b	Net unrelated business taxable income from Form 990-T, line 34	7b

			Prior Year	Current Year
Revenue	8	Contributions and grants (Part VIII, line 1h)		
	9	Program service revenue (Part VIII, line 2g)		
	10	Investment income (Part VIII, column (A), lines 3, 4, and 7d) . .		
	11	Other revenue (Part VIII, column (A), lines 5, 6d, 8c, 9c, 10c, and 11e) . . .		
	12	Total revenue—add lines 8 through 11 (must equal Part VIII, column (A), line 12)		
Expenses	13	Grants and similar amounts paid (Part IX, column (A), lines 1–3) . .		
	14	Benefits paid to or for members (Part IX, column (A), line 4) . .		
	15	Salaries, other compensation, employee benefits (Part IX, column (A), lines 5–10)		
	16a	Professional fundraising fees (Part IX, column (A), line 11e)		
	b	Total fundraising expenses (Part IX, column (D), line 25) ▶		
	17	Other expenses (Part IX, column (A), lines 11a–11d, 11f–24e) . . .		
	18	Total expenses. Add lines 13–17 (must equal Part IX, column (A), line 25)		
	19	Revenue less expenses. Subtract line 18 from line 12		

			Beginning of Current Year	End of Year
Net Assets or Fund Balances	20	Total assets (Part X, line 16)		
	21	Total liabilities (Part X, line 26)		
	22	Net assets or fund balances. Subtract line 21 from line 20 . . .		

Part II Signature Block

Under penalties of perjury, I declare that I have examined this return, including accompanying schedules and statements, and to the best of my knowledge and belief, it is true, correct, and complete. Declaration of preparer (other than officer) is based on all information of which preparer has any knowledge.

Sign Here	▶ Signature of officer		Date
	▶ Type or print name and title		

Paid Preparer Use Only	Print/Type preparer's name	Preparer's signature	Date	Check ☐ if self-employed	PTIN
	Firm's name ▶			Firm's EIN ▶	
	Firm's address ▶			Phone no.	

May the IRS discuss this return with the preparer shown above? (see instructions) . . . . ☐ Yes ☐ No

For Paperwork Reduction Act Notice, see the separate instructions.   Cat. No. 11282Y   Form **990** (2015)

The **Form-990 Summary and Signature Page** serves as a cover page to the submission. Note the filing is signed on this page by an officer of the organization, often the CEO (or the treasurer in large organizations). This signature is placed certifying under penalties of perjury that the filing is "true, correct, and complete." The IRS is serious.

Form 990 Part VIII Statement of Revenue

Part VIII	Statement of Revenue					
	Check if Schedule O contains a response or note to any line in this Part VIII . . . . ☐					
				(A) Total revenue	**(B)** Related or exempt function revenue	**(C)** Unrelated business revenue	**(D)** Revenue excluded from tax under sections 512-514

Contributions, Gifts, Grants and Other Similar Amounts	**1a**	Federated campaigns . . .	**1a**				
	b	Membership dues	**1b**				
	c	Fundraising events	**1c**				
	d	Related organizations . . .	**1d**				
	e	Government grants (contributions)	**1e**				
	f	All other contributions, gifts, grants, and similar amounts not included above	**1f**				
	g	Noncash contributions included in lines 1a-1f: $					
	h	**Total.** Add lines 1a-1f . . . . ▶					
Program Service Revenue	**2a**			**Business Code**			
	b						
	c						
	d						
	e						
	f	All other program service revenue .					
	g	**Total.** Add lines 2a-2f . . . . ▶					
Other Revenue	**3**	Investment income (including dividends, interest, and other similar amounts) . . . . . ▶					
	4	Income from investment of tax-exempt bond proceeds ▶					
	5	Royalties . . . . ▶					
			(i) Real	(ii) Personal			
	6a	Gross rents . .					
	b	Less: rental expenses					
	c	Rental income or (loss)					
	d	Net rental income or (loss) . . . . . ▶					
	7a	Gross amount from sales of assets other than inventory	(i) Securities	(ii) Other			
	b	Less: cost or other basis and sales expenses .					
	c	Gain or (loss) . .					
	d	Net gain or (loss) . . . . ▶					
	8a	Gross income from fundraising events (not including $ of contributions reported on line 1c). See Part IV, line 18 . . . . . a					
	b	Less: direct expenses . . . . b					
	c	Net income or (loss) from fundraising events . ▶					
	9a	Gross income from gaming activities. See Part IV, line 19 . . . . . a					
	b	Less: direct expenses . . . . b					
	c	Net income or (loss) from gaming activities . . ▶					
	10a	Gross sales of inventory, less returns and allowances . . . a					
	b	Less: cost of goods sold . . . b					
	c	Net income or (loss) from sales of inventory . . ▶					
		Miscellaneous Revenue		**Business Code**			
	11a						
	b						
	c						
	d	All other revenue					
	e	**Total.** Add lines 11a-11d . . . . ▶					
	12	**Total revenue.** See instructions. . . . . . ▶					

Form 990 Part VIII shows detailed revenue data from the organizations *Statement of Activities* (here called the *Statement of Revenue*). **Form 990-EZ** asks for similar information but in less detail. The **Form 990-N** (ePostcard) must be filed electronically and asks only if the organization's revenue is less than $50,000 in total.

Part IX Statement of Functional Expenses

Part IX   Statement of Functional Expenses

Section 501(c)(3) and 501(c)(4) organizations must complete all columns. All other organizations must complete column (A).

Check if Schedule O contains a response or note to any line in this Part IX . . . . ☐

Do not include amounts reported on lines 6b, 7b, 8b, 9b, and 10b of Part VIII.	(A) Total expenses	(B) Program service expenses	(C) Management and general expenses	(D) Fundraising expenses
1 Grants and other assistance to domestic organizations and domestic governments. See Part IV, line 21				
2 Grants and other assistance to domestic individuals. See Part IV, line 22				
3 Grants and other assistance to foreign organizations, foreign governments, and foreign individuals. See Part IV, lines 15 and 16 . . .				
4 Benefits paid to or for members				
5 Compensation of current officers, directors, trustees, and key employees				
6 Compensation not included above, to disqualified persons (as defined under section 4958(f)(1)) and persons described in section 4958(c)(3)(B)				
7 Other salaries and wages				
8 Pension plan accruals and contributions (include section 401(k) and 403(b) employer contributions)				
9 Other employee benefits				
10 Payroll taxes				
11 Fees for services (non-employees):				
a Management				
b Legal				
c Accounting				
d Lobbying				
e Professional fundraising services. See Part IV, line 17				
f Investment management fees				
g Other. (If line 11g amount exceeds 10% of line 25, column (A) amount, list line 11g expenses on Schedule O.) . .				
12 Advertising and promotion				
13 Office expenses				
14 Information technology				
15 Royalties				
16 Occupancy				
17 Travel				
18 Payments of travel or entertainment expenses for any federal, state, or local public officials				
19 Conferences, conventions, and meetings .				
20 Interest				
21 Payments to affiliates				
22 Depreciation, depletion, and amortization .				
23 Insurance				
24 Other expenses. Itemize expenses not covered above (List miscellaneous expenses in line 24e. If line 24e amount exceeds 10% of line 25, column (A) amount, list line 24e expenses on Schedule O.)				
a				
b				
c				
d				
e All other expenses				
25 **Total functional expenses.** Add lines 1 through 24e				
26 **Joint costs.** Complete this line only if the organization reported in column (B) joint costs from a combined educational campaign and fundraising solicitation. Check here ▶ ☐ if following SOP 98-2 (ASC 958-720) . . .				

Form **990** (2015)

Form 990 Part IX shows expense data from the organizations *Statement of Activities* and *Statement of Functional Expenses* by natural and functional class.

Part X Balance Sheet

Part X	**Balance Sheet**		
	Check if Schedule O contains a response or note to any line in this Part X . . . . ☐		
		(A) Beginning of year	**(B)** End of year

			(A) Beginning of year	**(B)** End of year
Assets	1	Cash—non-interest-bearing	1	
	2	Savings and temporary cash investments	2	
	3	Pledges and grants receivable, net	3	
	4	Accounts receivable, net	4	
	5	Loans and other receivables from current and former officers, directors, trustees, key employees, and highest compensated employees. Complete Part II of Schedule L	5	
	6	Loans and other receivables from other disqualified persons (as defined under section 4958(f)(1)), persons described in section 4958(c)(3)(B), and contributing employers and sponsoring organizations of section 501(c)(9) voluntary employees' beneficiary organizations (see instructions). Complete Part II of Schedule L	6	
	7	Notes and loans receivable, net	7	
	8	Inventories for sale or use	8	
	9	Prepaid expenses and deferred charges	9	
	10a	Land, buildings, and equipment: cost or other basis. Complete Part VI of Schedule D	10a	
	b	Less: accumulated depreciation	10b	10c
	11	Investments—publicly traded securities	11	
	12	Investments—other securities. See Part IV, line 11	12	
	13	Investments—program-related. See Part IV, line 11	13	
	14	Intangible assets	14	
	15	Other assets. See Part IV, line 11	15	
	16	**Total assets.** Add lines 1 through 15 (must equal line 34)	16	
Liabilities	17	Accounts payable and accrued expenses	17	
	18	Grants payable	18	
	19	Deferred revenue	19	
	20	Tax-exempt bond liabilities	20	
	21	Escrow or custodial account liability. Complete Part IV of Schedule D .	21	
	22	Loans and other payables to current and former officers, directors, trustees, key employees, highest compensated employees, and disqualified persons. Complete Part II of Schedule L .	22	
	23	Secured mortgages and notes payable to unrelated third parties . .	23	
	24	Unsecured notes and loans payable to unrelated third parties . .	24	
	25	Other liabilities (including federal income tax, payables to related third parties, and other liabilities not included on lines 17-24). Complete Part X of Schedule D	25	
	26	**Total liabilities.** Add lines 17 through 25	26	
Net Assets or Fund Balances		Organizations that follow SFAS 117 (ASC 958), check here ▶ ☐ and complete lines 27 through 29, and lines 33 and 34.		
	27	Unrestricted net assets	27	
	28	Temporarily restricted net assets	28	
	29	Permanently restricted net assets	29	
		Organizations that do not follow SFAS 117 (ASC 958), check here ▶ ☐ and complete lines 30 through 34.		
	30	Capital stock or trust principal, or current funds	30	
	31	Paid-in or capital surplus, or land, building, or equipment fund . . .	31	
	32	Retained earnings, endowment, accumulated income, or other funds .	32	
	33	Total net assets or fund balances	33	
	34	Total liabilities and net assets/fund balances	34	

Form **990** (2015)

Form 990 Part X shows assets, liability and net assets data from the nonprofit organizations *Statement of Financial Position* (herein called the *Balance Sheet* by the IRS for some unfathomable reason). **Form 990-EZ** asks only for total assets, total liabilities and net asset amounts.

Index

Further Reading & References

Greater Washington Society of CPAs maintains a useful website on the basics of nonprofit accounting. Probably the best place to go for additional information on finance and accounting for nonprofit organizations. Gives an interpretation of important nonprofit accounting concepts with greater detail than is in this book, but still highly readable. *(nonprofitacounting basics.org)*

National Assembly of State Arts Agencies is the membership organization that unites, represents, and serves the nation's state and jurisdictional arts agencies. NASAA's website is an excellent source of information about nonprofit accounting and financial reporting. *(nasaa-arts.org)*

Nonprofits Assistance Fund provides financial assistance helping nonprofits by answering immediate questions, increasing financial understanding, and aiding development of effective financial practices. You can schedule a telephone conference with them at (612)278-7180. Visit their website for useful information. *(nonprofitsassistancefund.org)*

GuideStar USA, Inc. is an information service specializing in reporting on U.S. nonprofit companies. Their database contains over 5 million IRS Forms 990 on 1.9 million organizations. A great place for comparative data. *(guidestar.org)*

Center for Nonprofit Boards is a leading resource for practical information, tools, and best practices, training and leadership development of nonprofit organizations.

BoardSource BoardSource publishes a series of useful monographs of particular interest to nonprofit board members and managers. *(boardsource.org)*

Internet Searches are very useful with ***investopia.com*** and ***wikipedia.org***. Type the site in the search bar and add the accounting term of interest. Surf the results and enjoy!

About the Author

Thomas R. Ittelson is the author of the best-selling for-profit accounting text, *Financial Statements: A Step-by-Step Guide to Understanding and Creating Financial Reports*. Now as a board member and consultant to nonprofit organizations, he brings his expertise plus a clear and informative writing style into the nonprofit arena.

Tom's audacious "mission" is simply to significantly increase the efficiency and effectiveness of U.S. public charities by improving financial literacy within those organizations. Immensely helpful information made accessible in an informal and witty way. No prior accounting knowledge is necessary.

Contact Tom at *ittelson@mercurygroup.com* for more information about his nonprofit financial seminars, work-shops, and board presentations ... or just to chat.

Other nonprofit books by the author:

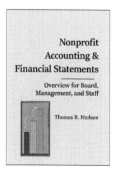

Nonprofit Accounting & Financial Statements: Overview for Board, Management, and Staff by Thomas R. Ittelson, 2nd Edition, 256 pages, 2017 (ISBN-13: 978-0-9971089-6-5)

A Picture Book of Nonprofit Financial Statements by Thomas R. Ittelson, 60 pages in full color, 2017 (ISBN-13: 978-0-9971089-4-1)

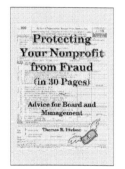

Protecting Your Nonprofit From Fraud in 30 pages: Advice for Board and Management by Thomas R. Ittelson, 30 pages 2020 (ISBN-13: 978-1-970050-01-1)

Notes

Made in the USA
Las Vegas, NV
17 July 2022